COFFEE CUP CHATTER

by Dominic. J. Zenden

Published by WriterMotive
www.writermotive.co.uk

Table of Contents

Introduction: Coffee Cup Chatter

We all have time to sit and chat with friends over coffee, our hopes and dreams stretching out in front of us as we share a cup that has been individually tailored to match our mood. Hot and sweet when tired, bitter and concentrated when we are ready to face the world, with our different moods manufactured in a cup. Coffee brings us together; it's the excuse we need to stop, it's the reason behind talking and sharing life experiences.

Life can be reflected in our habits; we can run our lives like we drink our coffee. Different moods for different days, different approaches for different people, we can also run around making coffee for everyone, if it makes them happy and totally forget about our 'own' needs!

Our relationships are the cornerstone that our lives are built on. Getting them right can lead to contentment beyond belief, get them wrong and we have to keep going around and around in circles, beyond frustrating. So where do we start to understand who we are? Well, our first place of choice is sitting down with a cup of coffee discussing our life or listening to our friend's problems. To understand who we are we have to get the thoughts from inside our heads to outside. When we constantly think about something it will drive us insane. Just talking about how we feel allows us to hear our own thoughts, share the thoughts of others, realise we are not alone in how we feel. So sharing a coffee with a close friend can be the best therapy ever. If we choose to keep our frustrations to ourselves we become volcanoes, something at some stage will push us off the edge, we will explode and end up doing something we may regret.

Understanding 'self' is the key to understanding relationships. Are we repeating the same behaviour time after time without even realising it, or could we be so uncertain about what we want we allow others to decide for us? The truth is the same for relationships as it is for any part of our lives - the harder we work at something, the better we get. If you want to fear or put no effort in that it will be what you get back, people who are so afraid or fearful or emotionally dysfunctional that any relationship won't work. The more effort you are prepared to put in, the better choice of relationships you will find. It's not enough to go in blind or with the opinion that others must approach you. This is your life, it's about learning the knowledge you need to make the right choices. By preparing to succeed you will, knowing the way to think you can avoid the pain and have so much more time to do the things in life that brings contentment.

For Alison.

Opening Thought

Coffee should always be served just too hot to drink, this isn't because I want you to burn your mouth but it's because it adds to the enjoyment of the experience. You should first smell the aroma, then feel the warmth through the cup as you lift it to your mouth, then the bittersweet taste as the liquid touches your tongue. Yes, I know it's just a cup of coffee but I believe we miss so much by just taking the experience for granted. You see life is like coffee, we all have different tastes and beliefs but we share the same sky. The more I look around the world, the more I see the same things. We have so many common day to day things that we all do, and share. So why in this age of media do we feel so disconnected? I think it's because we don't stop to enjoy or share. Once we start to think before we act, the world becomes a wonderful place to be.

Chapter 1: Self Matters

The most important person in your life is you. This is not being selfish or difficult. The key to your life is knowing who you are and what you want. Putting yourself first before others. Learning to say no. But how do we do this?

We all know who we are, don't we? We know the foods we like, what we like to do with our spare time, know the people whom we wish to avoid, know how we think about certain types of people, know the areas to avoid at night when we are out, we know so much. As adults, we have established who we are. Or have we? Do we need others to acknowledge us, praise us, speak well about us, do we want people to see us in a certain way, playing a certain role? Who do you think you are? Now I know these questions can be hard to answer, but knowing who you are is the key to being able to understand your own personal needs, especially when it comes to adult relationships. Let's start from the beginning.

From the very first moment you started forming opinions others have challenged you. We come to accept that our view is unique to who we are. But do we want to fit in? Sure we do. There is always safety in numbers, by agreeing we give away our own ability to make choices. Such is life! Our personal identity is already being moulded to what others expect from us, from the very moment we realise that we have choices; it's no wonder as adults we want others to come to us. So from the very start of our lives we are told what to do, and whom to play with. So how can we learn to go out on our own? I don't believe we ever do. I believe we can spend a lifetime wanting something different to what we already have, purely because we never have learnt how to make choices for ourselves especially in emotional relationships, the most important relationships we ever have to form. Not knowing is not a crime, thank goodness, but what it does is leave us open to those who can. Or those who think they can. Because we don't know ourselves, it's easy to go along with someone else. They can do the thinking for us! It's the lazy way to start a relationship. Very dangerous. It's unlikely to work unless you are a total doormat. It's why so many relationships fail, we both should be able to make choices, knowing who we are matters, think of it this way - if a person wants a relationship with you wouldn't it be good if they were interested in you. That might be stating the obvious but many miss this because they are so fearful of not finding the right relationship, not knowing where to start. A person who takes control can feel very attractive, they may talk about their life, their visions for the future, these will more than likely match your own because this type of people are very good at saying what they think you want to hear. It's easy for you, you don't have to say or do anything, you are just there a willing participant. Surely you have found your soul mate! Well, the reality is you haven't. Let's look at what is happening. A person has approached you. They have only shown interest in themselves, at no time have you been asked much about yourself. (This suits because you don't really know) You are happy to sit back and let this person do all the work. If you had a good clear understanding of who you are and what you wanted you would know that this person was only interested in one thing. A superficial encounter that was all about the chase, or they would be very controlling and deeply mistrusting. Not a good start to a lasting relationship. (I have met many people who have had no identity other than to want to please others that have found the people they have come to be with a nightmare), all because they didn't know who they really are.

So where do we start to understand who we are. Personal identity is the key. Knowing what you think, being able to believe in who you are. Having a personal understanding, start with your favourite foods, we all eat, then how you like to spend your spare time, learn about you. Spend some time on your own without doing one of the five things we can do without 'thought'. The five are: spending money or shopping, cleaning or housework, reading, watching television and finely studying, or learning. These are the five things we can do without including anyone else; I could include masturbation as a sixth but I won't! I'm sure you get the general idea. Hard isn't it? Start with your passions, the things in life you love or feel strongly about, your personality is in there somewhere just buried underneath a lifetime of doing what others wanted you to do, or never really thinking about relationships in this way before. What we are looking for needs to come from inside of you, not someone else, we know, we really do, it's just whether or not we really want to put the effort into ourselves, and why wouldn't we? It's not enough just to be there for others; it's not enough to accept bad relationships just because you never took the time to understand the real person inside.

Saying no takes courage, it's the opposite to the 'path of least resistance' - so many of us end up doing things we never wanted to do in the first place. This is not our fault. It's the fault of everyone we have ever met during our lifetime that has taught us how to behave around them. Emotional guilt starts young. Even children know how to get what they want by crying, as adults we tend not to use crying as a method, well the majority of us, we become more skilled in our approach. The power emotional guilt has over us is remarkable, just look at how you shop what you buy how many of us come across charity collectors without giving? It's all part of the emotional guilt which has been with us since very young. Relationships can be built around guilt so be aware of how the effects of not doing something make you feel, and how people manipulate us into doing what they want us to do. Saying no won't come easy. But it's always worth remembering you don't have to say anything. If you are unsure or you feel that you want to say 'no'; play for time. Never give an answer there and then. People who want something or need you to do something under pressure will always push you to doing what they want, praise you if you do, get angry if you don't (this is how people teach you to do what they want.) By not agreeing or disagreeing it gives you a chance to think about your decision, never ever ever make a choice under pressure, in life or in relationships.

Always do what is right for you. Understanding this one simple thing will give you back control of your life; you may never have to do something you don't want to again.

Thought

We are all winners. No matter what your place in society your life reflects your personal attitude. Believing you can do something is the basis everything is built on. When our minds are focused on a goal the 'goal' can be reached, the only thing we have to work out is the time scale. So the most important thing is having that thought in the first place. The thought is the trigger of the vision; the vision is a picture in our heads that shows us it's possible; once we believe than anything is possible. Now this is where some people fall down. It's hard for them to visualise, the thought is easy, but it becomes a distant dream because they don't believe. We can all be anything we want to be; we can all be winners, but the very first step is the realisation that a single thought can become reality.

Chapter 2: From the Start

Not moving too fast, how to spot the right people to get to know, our personal identity, who do we think we are? How others may see us.

Right from the very start of our lives we are learning. How to talk, we copy those around us, our likes which from an early age are personal. How do we fit into those in our world? What is our purpose? What role will be allowed to play? So many different dynamics are at play from the very start. I believe the hardest thing we learn is language; it's how we survive if we don't know how to communicate nobody notices us. This doesn't change as we go through life. The more we learn about communication the better we fit into our social surroundings, the more successful we become. So from the moment we learn how to speak by copying those around us the easier life gets. Well, I would like it to be this way. Unfortunately, it matters who we copy. Parents pass on the same bad habits or lack of understanding to their children. "Parent tapes" The things our parents tell us stick, go round and around in our heads forever, or until we learn how to erase these tapes with fresh information. Just because we have been shown or told does not make it so, but as children and then young adults we have little to compare what we are shown or told to. It's only when we meet people from different families or backgrounds that we discover it doesn't have to be the way we believe it to be. This can create conflict in our own minds; not knowing what is the right way to behave. It's hard to remove the knowledge we have gathered and replace it with a different way of thinking. Our parents are our first influence, not necessarily the best influence. This then asks the question "where do we learn about relationships?" Answer by making and breaking relationships. We only truly learn about adult relationships by being in them. Each person we date is different. A different set of values and beliefs that have been installed by a different set of parents or a different set of circumstances. We learn from our mistakes; that is if we are willing to take responsibility for dating the wrong person. So many of us blame that person for not wanting the same things, or blame them for letting us down by walking over our personal visions and dreams. It's so easy only to see relationships from a one-dimensional viewpoint, 'ours'. So much of what we think we are doing right isn't. We only believe it to be. So how do we start to unpick the minefield of adult dating? Like anything, it starts with you. We have no right to date. We have no right to think that others would want to date you. No matter who you are, what background you come from, all the relationships we ever create start with risk. Learning to manage that risk is the very first step in forming partnerships. Things that help us with 'the risk' are knowing who you are, and what you would like from a relationship. Being prepared to listen, and talk in the same amounts, and being comfortable with self-disclosure. (Having things that you are passionate about, likes, dislikes, conversational topics that represent who you 'really' are, not what you want others to believe you are.) If we show ourselves to be someone we are not, we will encounter people who are different to us. Being true to who you are is essential. A must for anyone wanting a long-term partnership. You are not ready if you first don't know what you want. Second are not prepared to manage the risk of meeting people. Third, want others to meet you. Fourth don't know who you are, or don't have any long-term visions for your life. Fifth expect others to make you happy, (If you are not content before you enter a relationship the chances are the relationship will let you down, or this will be how you see it). Sixth, if relationships are only a distraction from the routine of your life. Seventh, your moods are affected by how you feel about someone else (For instance if you get upset if they don't return your texts or S.M.S messages or phone calls). All of the above are things to work on before starting a new relationship. Prepare for successful partnerships and that will be what you will achieve. Sit back and just feel sorry for yourself without putting in the effort to prepare yourself you will get what you deserve, a bad relationship with a person who comes in like a speeding bullet and goes out as fast. This cycle is what people experience who give away their power not only to decide for themselves but also want others to do all the work for them. Why would anyone leave it to another? You are responsible for your own life; never ever think you're not.

With all that in mind how do we meet the right people? So many to choose from, so many emotions to cope with, and then we have our own pre-conceptions of how others see us. Something I came to realise is everyone is far too busy thinking about themselves to ever notice you. Just look around, people on mobile phones, reading newspapers, placing barriers up around themselves. Big signs saying 'Don't come near me', let alone talk to me! Then there are those who are constantly checking out how they look, twisting their hair into an imaginary place so it looks better, women playing with their makeup. I'm sure aliens would see this all as very strange behaviour. We accept it as normal! So, if others are so busy with their own insecurities there is no way they would ever notice us. As the world gets smaller we are becoming much more isolated from each other. We find it difficult to manage the risk of meeting others. Breaking down the barriers is becoming more difficult. This is why we should all know who we are. Without this knowledge how can we meet like-minded people? Being able to enjoy life, do social activities that we can relate to, if we don't know who we are this will never happen, (knowing who you are will put you in the same places as people like you, the very starting point of any friendship or relationship, if you meet people because they are doing what they feel good doing it's the start of having common thought, which leads to common visions). Another point worth consideration is when we meet a person it's rarely that we get to know them. Before entering into any relationship, we should always get to know their friends, their back story. Why do we rush? It's not like there is a prize for rushing into a physical relationship, quite the opposite. Those who have sex first then ask questions later are not hanging around, if you want that way of life that's fine but relationships are built on understanding not sexual urge. If you are getting this wrong then you are not ready for a shared relationship. Face facts. Don't blame the people you are meeting. Whilst on this subject, don't expect everyone you have sex with to want to repeat the experience. It can be the case that two people are just not sexually compatible, even if you may feel different. It's another compelling reason to get to know someone first. Learn about who you are and what drives you to do the things you do. No one ever forces you into any situation, and if you feel they might be forcing then the person is wrong for you. Again face facts before you act.

To get this across, think about people in three ways.

"The Hitchhiker" Easy to pick up, and then drop off. These people are often in a world of their own. Not interested in you, just your car! A fleeting encounter, which never in a month of Sundays would lead to a relationship. People who enter affairs will often encounter "The Hitchhiker" Full of what they want to do for you with no idea of how to. These people are stuck in their own world and don't have any intention of changing. Will feel sincere but never are.

"The Passenger" A person who just comes along for the ride. This person doesn't want to support you or care for you they just need to be helped through their life at that moment in time. This person is not interested in you. They are only interested in what you can do for them. Passengers are everywhere. The way to spot them is

simple. Talk about yourself. Then count the secon
your head before they turn the subject back to them. It's
good to realise just how self-centred they are. Passengers
make for very bad partners. You can never expect
anything from them. People who believe that by helping
and caring for others will lead to good relationships, end
up with "The Passenger"

"The Driver" A person who wants to share will take time
to get to know you, understand you and care for you.
You both have to know your destination to be in a
relationship with each other. These are the people to
look for. How do we know when we have found a
"Driver"? Simple, nothing is complicated; you find that
the issues can be resolved by communication. People
who get to know and understand first will meet
"Drivers" because they haven't wasted their time with
"The Hitchhiker or The Passenger" or have learnt from
the mistakes made in the past. Never rush into anything
that is going to last a life time. Take your time,
remember, it's only those with difficult emotional
moods who won't want you to get to know them. Never
make excuses for bad behaviour, and if in doubt walk
away. There will always be another relationship, value
yourself, make your own choices and always prepare
yourself to be successful when meeting new people.

Thought

We don't have to follow the crowd. We can set our own
standards. When we copy others, we lose some of our
own individuality. I have no problem with this; we all

do it. We dress in certain ways; we even follow the same events. The daily news is always about the same things. Choice is a strange concept. It was said that democracy is all about having choice. Well, that is true but we are still given who we should choose from. It's only a limited choice. So we don't really have the choice; we only think we do. Is too much choice a good or bad thing? I have seen people looking for ages at menus that hold so much choice. It's difficult to make up your mind. In short, choice is only good when you know what you want. This is why people tend to follow trends. It's easier to follow than it is to lead. Just look around if you go against popular opinion then you stand alone.

Chapter 3: Who are They?

The people we meet: what roles do they play in our lives? How much control do we have in forming friendships, relationships? What do others want from us? How do we know who is the right or who is the wrong to start an emotional relationship with?

Seven billion people in the world I find it hard to imagine how many that really is. We will only meet a few hundred during our lifetime; we should want to meet the interesting ones. But how would we ever know? What might be of interest to one isn't to another. So our starting place has to be 'who we are', we are unlikely to understand others if we don't come to understand ourselves. Language is one of our most outstanding skills. We take for granted so much about how we communicate. The words that we come to use, our phrases, and sayings become like old friends to us. It's like words can say anything we want them to. I believe if we want to change our world change our words. How we think is how we talk, so just by thinking in new ways we can start to use words to express what we really want, but much more than that we can change the way our life feels. We have all met the pessimist, either at work or within our families. Nothing is ever going to change, it's like these people are never happy. The words they use are in the negative, nothing is in their control, pure victims of everyone else. I know meeting these people is all part of life, but I would never choose to be in their company for any longer than necessary. They bring others down with them. If only they could change their words, life would become so much more.

This is why we must be careful what we tell ourselves. Whether we think, we can or we can't; we will be right. How we set out statements in our heads is how we will go about our lives. For example, how many people do we judge by how they look? We have already told ourselves what the outcome is going to be. Judging others before we have any real idea that we might be doing this. This is a big mistake to make. Why do we do this? It's all part of memory by association. The human memory is not that good in storing loads of information. The first things we remember is the negative, don't ask me why this is, maybe humans tend to remember the bad rather than the good, a form of self-protection from getting hurt or making the same mistake twice. Again this is wrong to do this on appearance alone. Appearance doesn't give us many clues to the personality, in fact, it can be so very misleading. Actors rely on us using association to character. Just think back to how many times you have been fooled by judging a person on looks alone? Many many times I would think. A good way of thinking is this. How many of the people in the past have you looked at by the way they dress and made hasty judgements? By the time you have got to know them how surprised have you become at who they really are? Either good or bad. I can tell you we never get it right, all because we already have preconceived ideas to who we think they are. Most of the people who we call friends we don't even look at anymore, we just accept. Avoiding this trap is one of the essential ways of meeting everyone on their merits. Don't be fooled by what you may think. Personally I love it when people judge me first. It gives me so much more to surprise them with. I could put on a white coat, this doesn't make me a doctor! Relationships can be hard enough. Meeting people is also difficult, why make it any harder?

If people are going to give themselves away it's normally by language. What people say is far more important than how they look. Our first impressions may not be the right ones. So what do we have to base our judgements on? Past experience, knowledge that we have accumulated since we first started to form relationships. Prejudice. The thoughts that others have implanted in our heads. Senses. How we feel about a person, instinct. There is not much else. As we get to know a person we have two ways of finding out more information. How the person themselves talks about who they are. How the person's friends relations talk about them. Our first contact is with them. One of the best ways to understand is to ask questions. We all know how to ask the simple questions, the very first thing we do is find out names, age and so on. We then establish common ground. Likes and dislikes, people we might have in common, where we live, places that we might have visited or lived. This common ground will allow us to move on to more intimate questions. Self-disclosure that is a little more personal, at this stage we have to believe what the person is saying, (a good thing to remember is - Don't ask the question if you don't believe the answer.) We can always check out the details later. Three questions to ask on a second date once it has been established that you want to be in their company are. "How do you get on with your parents?" Nice simple question that will tell you so much about the person. You are not trying to trip them up or catch them out. But the very first relationship we form is the one with our Mother and Father. It makes such a big part of our back story. All you should be looking for is honesty. Remember if this person is true you will get to meet the parents at first hand, you can at that point judge for yourself with the knowledge that you have acquired and remembered. This question is designed to help you understand the person. The next question gets a little more intrusive. "Tell me about your friends?" People in general have four or five close friends, and one of these friends is normally closer than the others. People who have long-term friends that they see regularly are on the whole good people. People with few friends or superficial friendships are often difficult. Again remember what you are told, and request to meet their friends. A person will not offer this if they have no intention of forming a lasting relationship. How people talk about their friends is also important. It's a way of finding out how loyal, understanding and trusting that person is. The back story of a person is a valuable aid into understanding who they are. The third question is now much more intrusive. "How did your last relationship end?" Now this is you. You could very easily be in this situation in the future. Listen carefully. The things that you don't want to hear are. 'They were very difficult to get on with'. 'They ran off with my friend'. 'We came to have nothing in common'. All these answers should wave a large red flag right at you. Relationships should always be uncomplicated, based on good communication and understanding for you and your chosen partner. Never forget the people we choose to share our lives with are the people who become to know us the best. All the above answers tell me that the person just jumps into relationships without getting to know, understand or even be able to match the needs of their partners. Be very aware of what you are getting involved in. So many miss these signs because they see in someone a person who has what they want. People with high profiles or money will often go through relationships because they can thus doesn't make them good partners. It just allows them to treat others in the way they choose without consequence. Without exception anyone who is still in a relationship even though they might say how difficult it is are liars. They have to lie to get you to be with them. If they can't move on before they have met you it's very rare that they will move on just because they have met you. Unhappy people are easy to meet. So many who don't know how to resolve, or move on, from bad relationships. This is not your battle or your war, please be honest with yourself and save yourself so much heartache. People who add in others before changing what they have are very stuck emotionally. These are the speeding bullets that we talked about in the first part of the book. Avoid these people at all costs, that is unless you like pain and even then you can buy a good pair of thumb screws that will inflict the same amount of pain. So you see there are all ways to hurt yourself. Never be fooled. Good answers for the same question include. 'I was wrong to be in a relationship that wasn't working for me.' 'My life changed so much it was hard for my partner to be with me.' 'I am a different person now to whom I was when we first met.' People do change, evolve into someone who holds no resemblance to the person they once were. These people are the brave ones; they face facts, look to change before moving on. Anyone who is looking to be in a new relationship must have dealt with the last relationship first. I always think of it this way. How hard is it to be with the same person your whole life?' Very! Those who achieve this are rare. There are those people who tend to have affairs then blame others for their own lack of courage, these are the people that add in others rather than face the difficulty of permanent change. The people who truly love each other I admire and respect but rarely meet. You don't have to sit and suffer no one should. Take responsibility for your life, learn to laugh and care about who you are, respect others, and never make others responsible for your own lack of courage. If it doesn't feel right the likelihood, it isn't. If you believe that tomorrow will be all right without changing today, you will be wrong.

Thought

Risk is a big part of life, how we manage the risk in our lives certainly changes how our life is.

Fear can stop us doing almost anything; the risk of failure or not achieving can be enough to stop us from even starting. Our thoughts are like well-trodden paths, we feel familiar with what we already know, it's a lot easier to walk the same route time and time again; very little risk of getting lost. So what happens when we take a risk? Sure we may fail; the risk may not work out, but it's getting back up and starting all over again. Millionaires have one thing in common they all failed at their first attempt, in fact, it takes on average seven attempts to get something off the ground. If you give up easily or dwell in the past mulling over your past failures you may always stop yourself. It's that well-trodden path again. Stepping into unfamiliar ground may feel unappealing but the rewards are there if you are prepared to manage the risk. The alternative is to live a safe life without much meaning or purpose.

Chapter 4: New Knowledge

Replacing the knowledge of times gone by. Challenging the conversational thinking of what it means to be "in love"

Do you live your life on the edge? If one more thing goes wrong, I'm not sure how I would cope? Or can you see things that are likely to happen and make provision for them? We all have choices, we can choose to plan ahead and figure out what might be needed, or we can just sit back and deal with what happens when it happens. Would you take an umbrella on a sunny day? Or would you just think well if it rains I will get wet? Both approaches are right and wrong. How often do you see people so laden down by all the things they carry? I call these the "What if people"! People who try to cover every eventuality, trying to solve every problem before it happens. Hard people to be around. Always finding problems to solve, and then when something does occur, it never happens in the way they thought it might, so they have to rethink, the energy these people take up with worry could be used too much better effect. Then the people, who don't care, live in the moment, take chances. Live their life on the edge. One thing goes wrong their whole life falls apart. Both extreme examples but we all fall somewhere in between the two. Balance, understanding, knowledge - keeping life simple will all help us cope when we need to find solutions. Being able to think in a different way can bring you new knowledge, knowledge that hasn't been apart of your upbringing or understanding. Until now, that is.

The only time you ever truly have is this moment. You can't change the past, the future hasn't yet happened. So if you want something it can only be achieved by starting now. Lose the need to know the future.' What if ' doesn't ever work. Let me repeat this 'What if ' doesn't work. Just hope it has reaffirmed this in your mind. It's part of your old thinking that has tied you in knots. Something else that has never worked either - comparisons. We can always find someone better or worse off than we are. If you find yourself looking at others and wishing, or feeling lucky it's false. The only person that matters is you, and what you have become. It doesn't matter why, that only clouds the situation. When we want to do something we will, it can be as hard or as easy as you believe it to be. As humans, we are lazy. We want easy ways to change. So why not choose the easy way? Maybe if we change would it be a reality that we don't really want? Those who want to change will. Those who don't want to change will talk about it, and then make excuses why they can't. But the real reason is they want to move on but doing so is so passed how they think, they can't visualise how life might be if things were different. First step into 'New Knowledge' is to visualise. Post up pictures, sayings that start to change how you are thinking. Learn some new words that you can drop into your daily conversations that reaffirm how you want to be. To change our lives first we have to change our thinking, to change our thinking we have to change our words, change our words change our lives. It's like anything that works 'simple'. "Today I would like to run 3 miles". "Today I'm going to run 3 miles". "Today when I'm hungry, I'm going to eat crisps". "Today I'm going to think about what I eat". Just two examples of how changing words, changes thinking, changes lives.

Replace those old sayings with new sayings. How we use language matters. We hold the same conversations with the same people every time we talk with them! This can become very boring, but easy. We don't have to think, just replay the same tape already inside. Try to change the conversations you have with people, draw something new into the exchange see what happens, start thinking about what you talk about, make the effort to notice how people find it so difficult to change the words they use, it can be very amusing once you start to notice. This is a powerful new way of thinking that you may have never thought about before. Writers of sitcoms will use these characteristics to get their audiences laughing.

Once you have mastered this it's time to look at the way you have come to think. So much of who we are is copied from our parents. This might not be that appealing to think about. I don't think I have come across many who like to think of themselves as clones. We might not even notice it, our partners are often the ones to spot it. It's natural to copy those who we live with, it's how we learn, doesn't make it right, it's just how it is. For years I would fold up the ironing board upside down, so would my older brother, this was learnt behaviour from our mother, it took my brother's wife to point this out! So if we copy without thought what else do we do? Just take a few minutes to compare just how much you are doing without thought, just because it's the way it has always been for you. The power of realisation will start to make you question why you think in a certain way. Our parents transfer their worries, prejudices straight on to us. Think past how you come to believe something. Rethink how you see the world. Each generation carries on to the next the way they think.

Emotional guilt. Something I have come to loath. It's a form of mind control. This is something once we realise how it works we can leave it behind. I would like to share with you some examples of how we can be made to feel guilty for being successful. We learn the early ways of how to understand relationships from the people who are the very first to affect our lives, our parents. The relationship they have is a role model for us, even if we don't realise. The happiness they feel or the sadness that affects them transfers directly to us. We will very likely create the relationship that they had into our own lives.

What is the last thing that we want to see when we feel unhappy? People having a good time. It's so hard to watch others doing what you want to do yourself. It just reaffirms that you are unhappy. Take this to the next step, think of a parent being unhappy then look at their children having successful lives. It's like the child rubbing it in. They can do what the parent can't. This scenario can create havoc in both lives. The parent will do anything to make the child feel guilty, will seldom praise or pass on compliments. The child then becomes distant because they want to feel good, something the parent can't bring themselves to understand. Then the parent will blame the child for not wanting to be in their company. This evokes emotional guilt. The cycle can go round and round. Don't let others bring you down. Be wise enough to see where that person is, tailor your behaviour or actions to limit how you project your life on to them. Remember the last thing we want when we are feeling down is an upbeat person telling us how good life is. This applies to family more than friends. Family can be the most difficult people to get on with. Accept this. Don't push, choose how you talk with them, you don't have to be friends but you do have to work out the best way of handling them. It's never personal although it may seem it. Parents / family have to be allowed for. Unlike friends you don't choose them, you just have to cope with them. It's very dangerous when people don't have consequences for their actions. In the parent, child relationship it's always worth remembering that parents can be rude, criticise or even put you down but they still remain your parents. This makes you an easy target. A safe person which has no rebuke. No, you don't have to be around them and you can choose not to visit or speak, but this is the last resort after all other methods have failed. Understanding what is behind their behaviour will help you distance yourself from any hurt. Knowledge comes in many forms, the new knowledge we seek comes from having the intelligence to see that when we copy it may not always be the correct way but if we only know one way it's not our fault. Learn to seek knowledge that hasn't been tainted with emotional guilt.

Thought

We all have our own personal opinions. Religion and politics will divide most of us. But how do we come to believe what we believe? You can break people down into three groups. Those who have an open mind and will consider the evidence in front of them. Those who wouldn't believe anything even if the evidence was right in front of them. And those who would believe anything even if the evidence pointed to something completely different. So how hard is it to have an opinion? Not all that. People tend to feel safer in groups. If the group believes then I'm on safe ground. Why should this be so? It is often those who go against the group that discovers 'The New Knowledge' that takes mankind forward. In fact without those of us who have gone against common opinion we would still be stuck back in the dark ages. Personal experience is everything as is the courage of your convictions. So whatever you believe in; believe in something that you know to be true.

Chapter 5: Smooth Sailing

When problems arise how do we solve them?

What sort of person are you? Let me give you a choice, are you - A silent worrier, everything inside, not wanting to bother anyone? Or are you a loud, I need everyone to know how I'm feeling person? Or maybe you are an ostrich, keep my head down, or if I don't see it I don't have to think about it? Or do you think if you help everyone else first your worries can wait? Or lastly, I'm going make everyone else's life hell until I get what I want?

Isn't it amazing we are all the same but so different? Each and every one of us can relate to the types of people above, I would think that most of us know someone that fits each statement. We may even admit to being one of the above ourselves. So how do we resolve problems? The very first step is working out who you are, and who the people are that you have alongside you. Each takes a different approach, so knowing that one solution doesn't fit all is the first realisation.

The key to understanding problem solving is - first knowing (what you want the outcome to be. Second - Who or what you are up against. Third - Using the right language. (This means preparation and not being sidetracked) Fourth, knowing that we don't have to be right, it's the outcome that matters.

I have heard it said in the past that God must have had a sense of humour when creating "men and women"! Emotional relationships do tend to prove this.

First please think carefully before feeling a problem has arisen. Most situations can be resolved with understanding, empathy and wanting what is best for your partner not what is best for you. Trust and honesty stand alone in building love and respect. If all your problems in your relationship boil down to lack of any of these then you might wish to rethink who your partner is, or why you want to be in a relationship with another person who can only see things their way.

Trust is a major part of any relationship. But how much do we understand about trust? Finding it hard to trust is common, it's learnt behaviour, not your behaviour. First in any relationship do not have sex until trust has been established. Joint visions must be established. Without them, trust won't start to grow. Problems are just around the corner. Close your eyes if you wish, but every relationship will be affected by how you feel. Never think that ignorance is an excuse. Learn the key things to understand before you enter a new relationship. Prepare for success. This will prevent problems. Far better than a cure.

Then next thing to understand is how people argue. Arguments only happen when you have a difference of opinion or different needs, or others want you to behave in a different manner around them. So many people teach us how to behave whilst in their company. We might raise a subject or want to talk about a situation that our partner doesn't. This can lead to problems. The thing to remember is if we have established common visions, then these situations become less likely. Before talking consider a few things. Is it the right time? Would it be good first to open the subject and ask when would be a good time to discuss it? This way we can prepare. If you just go headlong into something, the likelihood is the other person will be caught off guard. This isn't what you would want, not if your issue or problem is something that is bugging you. Reasonable people will act in a reasonable way. Never pick an argument just to get even. This will never work. The last word doesn't matter if you have been heard. If you haven't then it would be wise to question the relationship you are in, it is unlikely that it will change. Consideration is the key to relationships. Putting yourself in the other persons place is a skill well worth learning. The use of words is vital, I have never known another person to refuse to help if you ask them to. For example, key phrases like "Can you help me understand this?" or "How can I help you?" start a discussion on the right foot. Blaming or aggression will lead to defensive blocking arguments that just go round and round, like a playground dispute. "I think you're horrible.... You're horrible too" this is what I call the "Echo" argument. Save your breath, at no time will this sort of reaction ever resolve anything.

Understanding arguments is one thing, do we really need to argue? No is the simple answer. We only argue when we are either not heard or have a difference of opinions. Not hard to have a hassle free relationship, all you need is to listen. No, I mean really listen. Nobody wins when discussions get out of hand, we all want to be heard, we might not agree or get our own way all of the time, but hearing what the other person wants is a large step to finding harmony. The most infuriating people are those that believe they are always right. This is just an illusion in their own minds. You should never argue with an irrational person. You might as well blow up balloons! Use your breath for something constructive. Some common methods people use to win arguments are - Moving the goal Posts. It doesn't matter what started the argument, each time you raise and then defend a valid point they will just change the argument to another subject, or attack you in a personal way. These people would argue black is blue so they would never accept another person's view. In relationships, this type of person is a 'deal breaker.' Anything that you have come to establish with them can change in a second to suit their purpose or their argument. Be very aware not to be drawn into arguments with them, you won't win and you can become very unhappy because of the time spent understanding them is not reciprocated. Look out for this type of behaviour when you first meet it can help you avoid falling in love with a difficult person. A good thing to note in this area is family links. We learn how to stand our ground whilst growing up with brothers and sisters; people from large families can be prone to being self-defensive, not always the case, but we learn much from our backgrounds. Always find out about partner's families.

The Provoker. Those who provoke arguments just to get their own way or change the way a relationship is are easily spotted. These are the people who never know how to cope. They can come in and out of your life at will. When a difficult situation arises; they will pick a fight and leave. Normally because they can't support you during an emotional or difficult phase. They will never end the relationship. They leave the door open to return once you have gone through your difficulties. These are the people who want you because you can cope for them, not the other way round. In fact, these are again the "speeding bullets" we have talked so often about. Easy to find but very hard to live with. Relationships are about them. Anyone who comes in fast will go out fast and cause mayhem during their stay. Just think about how many people you meet are like this. If you are always meeting the emotionally difficult people it's because you don't know how to start relationships. Or you're in a rush to carry out your own agendas. When a person can only need from you and you haven't learnt to spot it you are in trouble. Arguments will become a daily part of your life which in turn replaces any joy you might have got from giving. Remember giving is two way. Think of it this way. You know that feeling you get when you give to someone? It feels so good doesn't it? So why wouldn't others who think the same way as you like giving to you? It makes them feel good too. So if you find it hard to take, or feel embarrassed by others helping you, rethink. It could be your own personal issue that is stopping you meeting like-minded people. Plus by allowing others to give to you, you are helping them feel happy! A win / win situation. Where's the problem?

When we argue no one wins. One or both are left feeling bad or unhappy. It is not normal behaviour, believe me relationships are at their best when simple. I love you, you love me. I want the best for you, you want the best for me. Working together should mean common ground, consideration pre-thought to avoid difficulties. Communication that is open and fair. I will listen to you if you listen to me. The one word I have left out of this chapter is compromise. We should never have to compromise in relationships. It's not about finding a solution, it's about preventing wanting to solve issues by talking. When we compromise, we lose so much of who we are and the dominant partner gets to have their own way. A relationship can only live on this for so long. If we get a "pay back" for example, marrying a rich person not for love but for what they can provide for us, we then can give up our rights. Our right to have a say, our right to control our own life, even our right to be loved. It is worth thinking about it if you find yourself in a relationship because of profile. It's funny how money can rule in a partnership. People can do anything they like or be forgiven for anything if money and lifestyle are the routes of the connection. If that's the only common ground you have then remember that you choose it. Money will never be and has never been a base to build a relationship on. But if that's what you want who am I to judge.

Thought

Shelter or Shadow. Two sides to everything. We can fear the dark or welcome the rest. We can use the cave as shelter or fear going inside because of the dark. It's only human nature to fear first. It's what has kept us alive for millions of years. But it's not enough only to see one side. Life in general is about balance, when we lose the balance our perspective goes. So how do we see the shadows? As a place to rest away from the light? Or as a place that may contain hidden dangers? The simple answer is both as a friend and foe. But how can that be? Everything in life is either black or white. We can't have it both ways. Or can we? By learning to live with an open mind, listening to both sides of the argument, could it be what we fear the most, is something that could be our best ally?

Chapter 6: Dating

This chapter is for all you single people. The knowledge you need to pick your way through the minefield of meeting, dating and living to survive the joy of a brand new relationship.

What is it about dating that changes how we see ourselves? In a day to day life we make good choices for ourselves, we would never rely on another person to make any choice on what we were about to build our lives around. So why should we when we date. Why do we have an expectation for others to find us? Could it be we don't want to take responsibility or the fear of failure overtakes us and leaves us without any alternative? It really doesn't have to be that way. Even if you believe in fate or soul mates it really doesn't matter. Your life is just that - 'Your life'!

So let's change some of your thinking. The most common misconception is we have to meet someone special. We don't! We just have to meet those who have common interests. (Now I know for that to work we have to know what we like, well if you're not sure of who you are then you're not ready to date, I don't care how old you are! Nobody is going to make you happy.) Self-identity is the most important thing to establish in your own mind. It doesn't have to be complicated; it just has to be yours. You might like cherry ice-cream, or The

Rolling Stones, you may find yourself drawn to certain groups of people. This is how we start figuring out who we are. The people we meet we don't have to date. So cut that physical attraction stuff out of your thinking. I wouldn't expect you to check out every person you come across; learn to make friends by sharing common ground. If you don't do this, you will build yourself up for so much rejection. It's not enough just to judge on looks. Get to know people, make friends without having to fancy them. It's amazing that so many want a short cut to finding a lasting relationship but are yet to learn how to understand themselves. If I sent you out to find that object I lost, without any description or location, you wouldn't know where to start looking! It's the same with dating, you need to know what you want first then you need to know what others may see in you. What makes you a good date? Have you dealt with your fear or your emotional issues? Are you prepared to fall in love? Or will falling in love bring back all the issues that you buried after your last relationship? I have met people who have protected themselves from relationships by eating and putting on weight so the opposite sex no longer desires them, a form of self-protection, it stops any emotional hurt. But leaves them feeling low and unloved. Most of us function better inside a relationship, especially if we take our time and get it right. The only question remains, where do I start?

I have already explained in this chapter about "self" it's the starting point for all relationships. Know yourself first. Simple I know but the way to meet people is to know what you like doing. If you don't know who you are you will meet "The speeding bullets" in fast, out fast. Or the hitchhiker or "The passenger", all of these types are ready to meet you right now, and then wreck your life. One fact that is hard for me to challenge is most people meet their partners through a second person. An introduction or by doing an activity that they both enjoy but have gone to independently. Common cause or common ground. That's why knowing what you like doing is so important.

Meeting people at work can come into this. Joint purpose both at work together, common ground, people in common, good conversational starters. All the right things together in one place. Ideal you may think. Well, yes many relationships start at work because of the very reasons stated above. But there is a 'but'. Be very careful. People can be very different people in and out of work. The majority of people we work with we wouldn't socialise with. Work brings people together but not necessarily the right people. If you do like someone you work with great, learn a little about them first, get to know them as a friend, discover if you have common goals, similar visions about life. This is always wise because we meet "The speeding bullet" at work too. And just what you don't want is a broken relationship and no job! Not a good combination. When it comes to workplace relationships, remember - 'there is no rush.'

Dating sites, social media. Why would anyone want to go on a dating site? Pure madness, but thousands do. In this age of instant everything, dating sites can offer a quick fix for those who don't have time to go out and meet people. Not a bad idea if you go in eyes wide open. Just because a person writes something in a profile doesn't make it so. Men lie about their height, women lie about their age. Men lie about what they want. Women lie about what they want. Do you get where this is going? People lie. Never take anything for face value. The photographs are either old or just head and shoulders. Did I mention people lie? Relationships that are formed on dating sites are very hard to establish, mainly because as soon as the first problem shows up the person is ditched and the other person is straight back on site. People don't want to work or stay loyal, well why should they? There is a whole list of people that they haven't yet met. I think of dating sites like a box of tissues. Take one out throw it away, take another out. If you have no expectations then go for it. If you are looking for a long-term relationship with a person who has dealt with their issues and has carefully considered your feelings, personality, likes and dislikes, 'Do not date online', it will end in tears. One last thing, people lie online 'Beware'

Get dating right and the rewards are amazing, I hope this hasn't put you off because I believe knowledge is the start of anything good that we do. You are here because two people took a chance and fell in love. It's not that difficult to do. The more you know and understand about yourself, the easier and more content you can become, Never expect anything, but want the most. Never undervalue who you are or the people you date. Manage the risk, it's worth it and never ever ever give up. Love is there for us all if we are prepared to work for it.

Thought

Your private life problems - please leave me out. Only you can work out your own problems. Others can guide you, even confirm what you are thinking but never make those life changing decisions for you. I'm a big believer that the truth will always turn up at some time. People will always show themselves for what they are. So if you ever have any doubts about a relationship wait, stand back and watch. Anything you need to know will be revealed. The beauty of life is that it is forever changing, as should we. It's not good to stand still for too long. The one area that should always stay the same is your friendships. Choose the right people and you will have friends for life. Good people make good friends. People without friends on the whole are normally difficult people.

Chapter 7: All I want is

In this chapter we take a look inside your personal thinking.

All I want is to be happy. This is a statement that I hear every day of my life. Without exception, the people who come out with those words have no idea what they are saying. You see happiness as an illusion, it doesn't exist. Sorry, but you will never ever be happy. If you set your goals in life in this way, you will forever be looking for something that just isn't there. In some ways, for some people, that can be enough. A self-fulfilling prophecy which comes true all of the time. So when we tell ourselves 'I will be happy when', if we are always changing what makes us happy, we are never happy. It's a classic way of thinking that allows us to want more and more without looking at the real reasons to why we need something to feel happy about.

Life is about what we feel from moment to moment. Our emotions can change in a second depending on what is happening around us. You can even feel this when a person walks into a room, the atmosphere changes. The same applies to any situation. Little words or actions can change the mood of the room. So if situations can change that quickly, so can we. One moment we would tell ourselves "I will be happy if" the next moment something else has become more important. This consent changing can be very confusing we have no idea what we are thinking about. No wonder we get lost in between loving and hating. It's a very thin line especially when in our minds we are telling our inner self something that isn't true. To get our thinking right, we have to go back to who we are. Think of yourself with nothing. No possessions, no personal needs, no hunger or thirst. You are just energy that exists to learn. A blank canvas just to experience. All your human "wants" have long left your consciousness. What would this feel like? Bliss, no fear or worries, no 'if onlys'. Well, the truth is you were once like this. Before you were born, you had everything you needed to grow. Your mother provided for your needs just by being there. No conditions were placed on you. You didn't have to say or do the right thing. The only consequence was that the moment you came into the world, you would start to be exposed to human life. Emotional guilt, the need to ask others, the need to get on with others, the fear of failure, being judged, not knowing. All of these very difficult new things to learn about. What chance did we stand? So over time we grow, we conform into what we are told to do and watch how those around us do the things that we someday would like to do. From the very start of our first breath, we want to do something we can't. So why should this change as we get older? I don't think it does. I think it's this inner programming that makes us want things that are slightly out of our grasp. We tell ourselves "I will be happy when" but don't really mean it, is just so ingrained into how we think it would be hard to imagine life without wanting something. It's how we survive. It's how we recreate what has gone past. We just fit into a world where we all are expected to want something. "What do you want to be when you grow up?" A very common question that we are asked throughout our early lives. However would we know? No wonder child copies its parents, it's all it knows. On one hand, we are told not to question on the other hand we are bombarded by questions that we may not be equipped to answer. So from those early moments when we are first conceived to the growing up years to adulthood we are expected to know what we want. Could it be just all right to want nothing? In the world that we live in wouldn't it be strange if you asked another what they wanted and they answered "nothing, I'm just happy watching the wheels go round". This is so far from how we are taught to see the world that others would think of this as being unusual. We are taught that ambition is the foundation of a happy life. Not true. When I was sixteen, I thought I needed to be someone. It wasn't just enough to go to work draw a wage. I needed to be ambitious, it wasn't enough just to pack books, I should want to be the warehouse manager. This was until I met Paul. Paul was in his fifties, a kind polite man with a family. He came to work doing the same job as I was. Being sixteen I was curious, I couldn't work out why a man of his age was working in a job that offered little in the way of promotion or prospects. His answer was simple. "I have what I want from life, my wife, my home and daughter, I don't need for anything, I'm content. Work is just a means to an end. I come to work do my job go home, no worry or need to think it's bliss". It took me a long time to get what Paul said to me that day, about thirty years in fact. I wish I had listened more carefully it would have made my life a lot easier. We all find our own levels. What we want and what we need are two very separate things. Being content is the key to a "happy" life. Wanting what we have, not having what we want.

Relationships can ever only be lived in the moment. If all you think about is wanting something new, a different relationship, a new car, a bigger house, you are not content. Contentment means that you don't have to desire to feel good inside. Quite the opposite, the more we live with what we have, the more we can enjoy the moment. Our minds become uncluttered, our focus clear. As I will always say: uncomplicated your life. Lose the need to think you need. Lose the need to know the future. It just complicates how we think and feel. Get your thinking right change your life.

Thought

Wishing I was lucky. We all need things to fall our way, but does luck play a part in the way our lives unfold. Well, it may. But it's far more likely that our own destiny is very much in our own hands. Those of us who succeed don't do it first time around. It will take much effort to achieve our own personal goals. Life is all about getting back up if at first we fail. Those who do; create their own luck. By preparing to be successful, you will be, it's just a matter of time. My message to you is you can be anything you want to be if you take personal responsibility for your own choices. Being ready to take opportunities at all times, never turn down a chance to shine.

Chapter 8: You can go your own way

Why would others want to control us or teach us things that are untrue? Whose truth is it anyhow?

Are my needs any different from yours? Well, I would think with a few exceptions we would both want the same things. This is quite a thought, no matter whoever you are, your back story, your individuality or personal circumstance we can agree that we both need the same things in life? So why isn't everyone more tuned in with each other than they are? It's because we all believe our needs are individual to us personally. This is just untrue. We may wish it to be so. We might even construct an argument to debate how your needs come before mine, but when everything is taken into consideration, we all live under the same sun. We would survive if the world suddenly went back a thousand years, some of us better than others I grant you, but the truth is we all have the same emotions, we all breathe the same air just some of us would like to think we are more deserving than others.

This thinking is a part of our culture, no matter what culture we belong to. Wars have been fought over different countries believing that their people's needs are more important than the next country. Understanding that we all have the same needs is the first step in working out why people would want to control us.

There is no truth. There is only your version of how you see the truth. This is so right across history. Or just in your own life. How we recall circumstances and events is our own personal view. It's what we have come to believe not the way it was or might have been. Whilst you think about that for a while lets discuss how our own version of the truth affects our close relationships. No matter who we find ourselves with we will still have the same needs. So do they. We can choose to learn about their needs or we can teach them our way. Most relationships are based on need. So the first thing we do when getting to know a new partner is use "self-disclosure" this is always from our own personal recall of events in our own life. Doesn't make it "the truth" just makes it our truth. Worth remembering that we are very quick to change our own version if it doesn't suit our personal picture of who we are. As humans if we recall an event we want to change we would enhance the story, make it more the way we wanted it to be. I always find it fascinating listening to two people recalling a series of events in their own words. It is said that you have to take what is said and in the middle somewhere is what really took place.

So let's now talk about truth. This is a part of this book that you may wish to skip, if you are so fixed in your own way of thinking, it might not even be worth me offering you a different way of thought. The way you are has got you to this point in your life, why change?

Well, first understanding your own mistakes will help you open your eyes to your own personal behaviour. Do you find yourself on your own thinking about the way things really happened? Even in your deepest darkest nights the truth remains with you however you wish to recall it to others. You don't even have to acknowledge to others how you see yourself, it's private. For your mind only. No one can see into our thoughts, can they? But you have to live with the consequences of your deeds and actions. (One thing to consider is we all change the truth, so even if you have changed something in your own mind, it doesn't affect anything, only you. You are far more likely to repeat your behaviour if by stating to yourself that you were justified in behaving that way.) Nothing will change, you will go round and round, repeating the same mistakes, blaming others. Everyone has a tipping point. You will discover this as you go through life. You will find it hard to make friends because you are only loyal to yourself or when it suits. Friends won't hang around; it might take some longer than others, but the end result will be a life of isolation, false truths and lies. All because you couldn't accept the way your life is. It's a tough path to walk, because by blaming everyone else you are very unlikely to change. Why would you? You're never wrong.

So even if you think about this yourself, in your private time, in your head it may help you as you move forward. No one has to know, by taking responsibility for who you are, you can release yourself from the "beartrap" of life. No rush, you may like feeling upset and angry at others.

The beginning of who we are is being honest. I have never met a person who will admit to being dishonest, they will dress up their deceit in lots of different words. Words like "If I didn't do this somebody else would." "They deserved to be treated in this way, they let me down." "Disloyal people should suffer." All these. They are angry at something or someone. Living in a prison cell in their own minds, carrying the sins of others and spreading their vile poison everywhere they go.

Crazy life. Doesn't have to be that way. I believe we get the life we deserve. Not because we can be successful if we work hard but because if we face how things are or where we can leave them behind in the past. People are not perfect. That means us too. Why should we expect others to act in a perfect way towards us when we don't even know who we are? When we discover the value in truth, real truth, no embellishments or versions that suit our story, only then can we life with true peace.

Think about this way - We all want a good life, but what does this mean? It means no confrontation, it means having enough not to have to worry. It means being able to share our loves and passions with other liked minded people. We call these people friends. It means being able to accept that others may see things differently. This is not making allowances, this is pure acceptance. Empathy is something everyone talks about, few have it. We would all like to think we have it, like not looking our age, we would all like to think as ourselves being younger, but the reality is most of us look the age we are, unless we choose to try and fool others by dressing up, or dying our hair or in this modern world; cosmetic surgery, it fools no one we all know how old they are. You may fool yourself, falsely believe that others see you in the way you want them to. Empathy is only apparent when we know what the other person is experiencing. Few of us know, most of us don't care, as long as we are alright. Which in turn takes us back to the truth. If it doesn't affect who we think we are or impact into our lives, we can very easily make up how we want it to be.

One last comment on truth. Because truth is just a version that others accept as being what happened, it doesn't matter. The only thing that matters is how we are prepared to live. Are we prepared to live with always wanting, wanting life to be different, wanting others to treat you differently, wanting to understand the truth? This all starts with you, it's in your own personal thinking too.

Thought

A brand new day. Exploring new places for the very first time can be a little daunting, unfamiliar areas that hold hidden surprises. It's easy to stick with what you know, it takes very little effort. To come away from this though has its rewards. You can forget who you are, surrounding yourself with people who already know you is very safe. But I believe you get from life what you are willing to put in, strangely enough it's amazing how many people will put themselves out for you but only if you make the effort first, it's like a test. What I notice, is actions that take effort are rare in others, so when people travel a long distance just to meet you it's a big compliment, they have spent their time travelling because they think you are worth it.

Chapter 9: Breaking The Chain

Being able to see clear enough to know it doesn't have to be that way

The best way to understand anyone is to look at their past. Parents, siblings, schooling, relationships are all a part of our past. The very start of our understanding. No matter what age we are, we all look at life from one perspective, our own. Most of us can recall childhood memories when we can remember feeling very alone. I think this is common to most of us. Our world is just the people closest; we can never imagine what it would be like if it was different. Our parents are the only parents; we have no way of comparison, it would be reasonable to think that all parents act and talk the same, wouldn't it? I can remember the shock I got in my early years realising that different families had different types of parents. My first shock was when a friend's dad came out and played football with a group of us. My dad would have never done this; it was fantastic, and very different to what I had experienced in my own family. I can recall thinking that if I ever had children I would make the effort, break the chain, it didn't have to be the way it was for me. That one realisation is the start of working out that you can go your own way; parents don't have to be role models. We could learn from everyone, no exceptions. It just so happened that my parents were not that good at being parents. Looking back I now know this; hindsight is a wonderful thing, but because they were like they were I chose to learn about people. I learnt the one golden rule "life is only as good as you make it" No one can make your life for you." It's true that others can look after you, feed and clothe you, interact with you, punish you and place their prejudices onto you. But no one can be you. Your past is like a window to your soul. Every lesson that you have ever learnt, everything that you have ever got wrong, your memory is fantastic tool to punish, time and time again. Who needs others to reconfirm who we think we are? We live with ourselves every moment of every day.

From this, we can choose to learn and change, and if we do we can look back at certain landmarks in our life as turning points, lessons learnt, remembered and then moved on from, picking up the pieces and starting again. This is our personal chain of memory. Understanding the past is more or less important depending on who we blame for the way we think. No blame, no need. Blame then need. We are all wired differently which makes us all individual. But working things backwards is no answer when all we want to do is move forwards. Does it really matter how we got to be here in the now? Not really. Let go of blame, hurt and confusion. It's true that you may never understand "Why" There might not even be a reason. It just could be that your parents were not very good at being parents either. Throw away the need to blame, work with what you have, "You". When a watch breaks you don't keep watching it hoping it may start up again, or that it might by some miracle start again at the right time! You have to mend it and reset the dial. We are like watches. Set the right setting and it will always tell us the truth, we would never be late for anything, however put the wrong settings in then what do you get, misleading information that is constantly wrong. Our parents are the watch setters. We are the watches. It's true, we may need to be reset with the correct information. Only the information we need is how to see life, whilst working out what type of person we are.

When you meet a new person, you have no idea who they are, you have no idea if they are truthful loyal, understanding. All the judgements you make will be based on three things. 1 The things that they tell you. 2 The questions you ask them. 3 The things they don't tell you. You have to rely on these three things until you get to know them well enough to meet their friends and family. (If by some chance you never get to meet these people then the person is hiding something from their past, so it's worth considering meeting a more open person.) The persons past will give you a far better idea to who you are dealing with. I always keep it in mind that people are not bad, but may have done bad things or been around bad circumstances. Again their chain of life events is a good place to look. We all have change written in at certain stages. Affect and course. We change for many reasons. What we are looking for however is repeat behaviour. Making the same mistakes time and time again. This is a strong indication that they either can't change or don't wish to change. I see the same behaviour in people who find commitment hard to give. They start relationships, go along until challenged then move on to the next relationship. (Dating sites are a good place to find people like this.) It all comes from past behaviour, learning the wrong settings from a parent, it's a way of life for them. If it's not your way of life give these people a wide swerve. This is one example of how past behaviour can be an indication of future behaviour. You will also see the same patterns of people who carry around addictions. A stop-start lifestyle that takes so much effort. Constantly moving on from relationships, covering up the past and carrying on their addiction, it's a cycle that is easy to spot. These people are drowning in their own lives. Of course, you can choose to help, stick around make life easy for them difficult for you, with no guarantee of a positive outcome. Something to consider is this. People who go through an emotionally difficult time will often look to add people into their lives just to support them. Once the difficulties are over they move on. This is because they don't want to be reminded of the "old times"; who they have been. No loyalty to you. Just a person who wants to erase the memories of the past. You would be one of those memories. If you see yourself as an emotional fixer, or a person who is stuck attracting emotionally difficult people to you, these are the people that will find you. Understanding their chain can prevent much heartache.

In this chapter, we have talked about some of the basic ways to discover who someone really is. If all you want from life is to be an ostrich that's fine. One step at a time, fall in love first ask questions later, that's all good too. You have it in you to think in a different way, to question, to ask to meet friends and family, not to take things on face value. This isn't a trust issue this is looking after yourself. You would never buy a car from another person without asking questions or even taking it for a test drive. People lie. I know that's a hard thing to believe. But they do, When you look at that shiny bodywork, all buffed up, the car may be very appealing, but when you lift the hood if there is no engine or the exhaust is falling off, or the tyres are bald or the service history is not shown or the car has had many previous owners you are not going to invest in that car, well not if you value your money. Relationships can so easily be seen in the same way.

Thought

What do we really worry about? The future? What may happen when? We can always find things to worry about in our own lives, and when we run out of worries we just turn our thoughts onto others or world affairs. Now it's always good to have concerns about issues that are not right. The world has many things ongoing that we can think about whilst making others aware of. But life is beautiful, every moment precious so why do we get caught up in stressful thinking? I believe it becomes a habit; We don't know another way. Just look at the media, full of negative "news" stories. Good positive relegated to the bottom of the page. Just recently a lady asked me to read for her but she didn't have the money to pay my fee. No problem. I promise to do a 90 minute reading for her with one condition that she passed on the time I had given to her to someone else. I wanted her to help another person. Start a chain of positivity. It's the way forward. Let's help each other. Rather than worry about how something is going to happen.

Chapter 10: Let's talk about Sex

What happens when the male and female worlds collide.

Men and women are different! This may or may not be a surprise to you, but I doubt if this information will rock your world. But understand why the different gender's think so differently may help you understand what makes us as humans tick.

Before we get into the "Nuts and Bolts" so to speak, it a good place to start in acknowledging that sex can be the most fun that we ever have without laughing, in fact, you can have sex with anyone. You don't even have to know anything about the person; you don't have to talk with them, understand them or even support them, sex can be a unique event that two can share without ever having to know anything about the person. Maybe that's why so many people do have sex with strangers. No need for clever conversation, or expectations, just pure sex. This is easy. And I suppose the real reason why the human race has survived for so many thousands of years. If sex was difficult, or unpleasant, do you think we would go to so much trouble in pursuit? No way, the human race would have died out before it began. So sex is a natural function for all of us no matter what is said or how it is portrayed sex is the most normal and wonderful thing we can experience in our adult life.

So why do men and women see sex in such a different way? Well, the simple truth is we don't. We both have the same sexual needs. If it was just about pure sex then men and women would both agree, it's about what happens next.

Although there is only one reason we have sex, the implications of sex are vast. What we must understand is what does it mean to have sex with another person.

For this we need to go back in time, so far back we would be living in caves, the very beginnings of the way we started out. We tend to forget our past. The reasons we were able to reach this stage in our evolution as a race.

This is how I see the different roles we play in the aftermath of sex. In the Stone Age, man was responsible for his and her own survival. The male was the hunter, the provider. His role was to hunt, gather food build shelter find water; this was not argued about it was his purpose. The stronger or fitter the male was, the more partners he could provide for the more likely he was to be a desired male. The alpha males would compete for the attention of the females. He had to win the right to have sex, not by what he said, but by his deeds or actions, a good hunter could provide for many females, this meant only the strong survived. The weak males who could not hunt and fight were soon lost to the gene pool. Hence we became a race of fit and strong people. This was how it was meant to be. I don't believe we were ever just meant to mate with one partner. (This would come in many years later with religion and control by the churches) See men were not made to be what we know today as "faithful" in western culture, it was never their intended role. The natural selection of evolution would sort this out for us, and it was for the benefit of the species. We made it through thousands of years this way. So let's skip forward to modern man. He no longer needs to hunt and fight if he doesn't wish to, but the modern day female is still attracted to the alpha males, with all the implications this involves. We live in a society that has created the family. This is a female concept. Let's jump backwards one last time. The cave woman. Her role was to have children, feed them care for them. She wouldn't need for much; just shelter, food and protection (no change really to modern times). Her role was to reproduce the future generation. The male would be far too busy hunting and fighting to play much of a role in the children's early progress. So a woman's instinct is to look for a man who can provide for her. Those females who were successful in finding such a male would have children, and the circle would continue. This is where are needs comes from. Understanding this does show that although we may be technically aware in these times we are not emotionally aware. The true order has been switched around so much that we don't know where we are when it comes to mating. Our minds are so mixed up because we don't have to fight for the right to mate. Anyone can have sex with anyone, this by itself will bring the human race down, because we don't have to be the strongest or the fittest we can just be. The gene pool is now full of faulty genes that build imperfect human beings. Now before you start running of into your own conclusions. People don't have to be perfect, nor do they have to be the brightest to survive, I know that's true as long as medicine keeps up. If we can resolve the issues we have created by fixing them, then it will be alright to have sex out of order. We still need to understand why men and women act the way they do. Men were never made to be faithful; women were never made to mate with weak males. What I'm against more than anything is the emotive words people have come up with to describe relationships. "He cheated on me" "She's a tart" This finger pointing is far too easily used in our relationships. If we were meant to be in a one to one relationship it would come natural, we would do it by instinct. We wouldn't even think the way we do. The reason we have so many emotionally difficult people / relationships is because we are going against the way we evolved. So knowing this, how can we live together without coming up against problems?

We have a vital edge; we have learnt to talk. To make relationships work in the 21st century, we must talk. Because we need to share the same visions to stay to together, we must exchange what it is we want from our mates. The person we decide to have sex with must know what our intentions are. Are we prepared to work together for a common purpose? If so then let's have sex, if not then move on. The difficulties only arise when we have sex before our intentions have been talked about. Simple - don't have unprotected sex with a stranger. Easy. Doesn't have to be mind-blowingly complicated. I think we can all grasp this. In these days that we live in freedom is an amazing thing. We don't have to have children with anyone! This is an amazing fact that has only ever in the history of mankind been available to us. Yes, we are the first to be able to have a guilt-free sex life. No responsibility or worries, have sex with whoever you want to, go around the world, mix with different cultures and sex yourself silly, if you really want to. But before you do make sure your mind is in the right place, don't fall in love, and don't become needy of anyone. Your choice is to be who you want to be. But if you want a long-term relationship, fall in love and raise children, live with the same person for 60 years grow together, understand the security of a long-term partnership; for men you may need to curb your natural desires to chase anything that you can just because, and women you may need to give your men a little leeway, it's worth it.

We are all the same. We can't deny how as a race we have evolved. Not sure everything we have today makes life any easier than it did for out distant relations way back in time, it's just different problems. One solved another created. I believe in progress but with progress comes responsibility, if we want to live in freedom then we must play by the rules.

Thought

I love the world we live in. So many wonderful people in the world all doing their best to help fellow humans achieve, it never fails to amaze me how many want to offer you some kind of help or improvement that would enhance your life. Then there are those who seek you out because you may be able to help them. For me, I would rather put people first. Helping others is a natural thing. But I always remember that we should give others the tools to help themselves. When a person is prepared to work hard it makes it an easier job to help them. When others sit back and expect then no amount of kindness or help will affect the outcome. With the best will in the world, kindness will never work if they don't.

Chapter 11: A state of Mind

In this chapter we will explore what we think of ourselves and how this affects how we see others.

What makes one person successful and another not? Could it be how we think affects our lives in a far deeper way than we could ever believe. So where do our thoughts come from? The simple answer is we just don't know. A spiritual teacher might say your thoughts come to you from many different sources. But we are like sponges, everywhere we look we can find inspiration, so many would like us to think the same way they do. It can be very easy to read a book or watch a television programme coming away believing it's the truth. It's not; it's only the truth as the author sees it and how the producer and director have interpreted it. Think about how many different people would like to get inside your thoughts. It's the key to making lots of money. Make you believe you can't do without something then a multi-pound industry will spring into life. Supermarkets, fashion shops, entertainment all rely on getting inside your thoughts. Powerful.

So how do we control what we think? Like anything it's simple. We must be aware of the way we think. Everything we will ever do has to have a "pay off" If it doesn't we won't do it. The state of mind we find ourselves in will affect the choices we make. We want to be thinking that way at that moment. Our moods play a large part in our behaviour. This in turn moulds the way we think, what we believe we need. Advertisers would love us to associate our different moods with their products. So be aware of this. Your true needs are simple. Food, water, love and shelter. Everything else comes in ascending order depending on how we think and what our personal priorities are. We really don't need very much at all.

What is it with some people; they seem like they are enjoying life, they have what they want in life. Could this be connected to the way they think?

Sure. If you believe you can or you can't you will be right! How could that be? Why would self-belief make this much difference? Is it a state of mind that makes people successful? Let's explore how our thinking works. From an early age, we are taught how to think and behave. If we are taught that life is meant to be difficult, we will believe this until our clock is reset. (Chapter 9) So this is how we think. Nothing good will ever happen so why bother. So we just don't put ourselves out. On the other hand if our parents are dynamic we are likely to follow their example. Our thinking is led by first who taught us in our early years, not necessarily by just words but by actions; we pick up far more by watching than we do by listening. Then our personal situation and needs. If we find ourselves down without anything, no relationship, or money it's how we react to these circumstances. How we react is very often pre-programmed, our deal has already been set, rightly or wrongly. The knowledge that life doesn't have to be the way it is can change your thoughts. Get your thinking right change your life.

With this in mind not everyone can be successful, or even want to be, but one thing that those who reach the top have in common is the will to never ever ever given in. This applies to relationships as much as business. It's very rare that a person makes it first time. It's how we react to failure that will create the path that we follow. Could you ever imagine still being with the first ever person who you dated? All the mistakes, the things that you would do differently now. Life is a learning curve. How quickly we fix the things that we get wrong matters. If we think we are doing right because that's how we learnt to do, and it isn't the right way, at some stage we would recognise that our thinking is wrong. People who can change will often realise sooner rather than later they have based their judgement on wrong information. I find it hard to understand people sometimes. If our car is going wrong we will take it to a person who knows about cars to fix it, we wouldn't try to do this on our own would we? So why when the mind has the wrong thinking and life is going wrong why don't we seek out those who know? We just don't want to, do we? We believe we can fix ourselves, or just act like a victim, never expecting anything to get better. How we think affects the life we get. By giving in easily, we may never know what it is like to be successful. If we believe this was always going to be the way of things then we have proved ourselves right, well done! A life of underachievement is your reward for believing you can't. In a survey of millionaires, not one of them made it first time, in fact on average it took them seven attempts to create the lifestyle that they have today. Seven times of picking yourself up off the floor, seven times of overcoming disappointment, seven times of getting it wrong and learning from the experience. Seven times just think of how many times you have given up after just one attempt? The people who become successful in life have some major thinking on their side. They believe in themselves; they don't let others tell them they can't, they don't let disappointment get in their way, they handle rejection and move on to the next. How simple is that? It's no secret. One thing they will have in common is this; they have either had parents that care enough to set good examples, or they have fixed their thinking first. The thought of achieving hasn't scared them it has motivated them.

We all have our very individual ways of looking at life. Our thinking starts from watching others, learning what does and doesn't work for us. Some of us will just keep repeating the same behaviour; these are the people who will always believe what they see to be true. This is like painting a picture in only two colours when you have the whole rainbow of colours to choose from. If we believe it to be, so it is, well it is for us that way. Take your thinking out, allow yourself to see life from many different perspectives. Consider what you don't know not just what you do know. If something challenges your belief structure go with it, you might find a different way that is better. So many of us want a safe life. Your thinking would be safe at all times, never take a chance, speak to a stranger, read a book that may conflict with your thinking. How would you ever grow? How would you ever change your thoughts if you don't challenge yourself? This is not the easy way. The safe way is a lot harder than you may ever have thought. People who never challenge themselves stand still, find things to complain about, criticise others who take risks and expand their knowledge. "If I can't do it, why should you?" Believe it or not the reason safe people do this is to make up for the lack of self-belief. It's very safe to criticise; it's easy to fill the gaps in your life by finding fault, it covers up the space in your mind that is designed to take chances or to push yourself to the edge. Just because your dial has been set to the wrong time! Finding fault is easy. We can find it in everyone and everything we come across. It's the best way of not having to change yourself. "Everyone else is wrong." Just think how good life is! Just think how a small change in your thinking will change everything. Don't believe me? Just try it, like all things in life it's simple.

Thought

The very beauty of being mortal is that we all are unique, and have the ability to make our own choices, our own opinions, and this should be celebrated. When we copy others we dilute who we are, we lose some of our uniqueness with a consequence that we lose our own individuality. All because we are too lazy to put what we truly think into our own words. We choose to copy what others have said or done before us. If we want to be truly unique, which we all have the capability of, we should use consideration of our own thought beliefs to share with others what we believe in. Do not adopt the thinking of another. The very reason I publish my own unique thoughts daily is to create a place where others are truly free to express their opinions. Without this exchange, we could never grow.

Chapter 12: Golden Rules

In this final Chapter we bring everything together in the 7 Golden Rules of relationships.

Golden Rule One: Don't take yourself too seriously

Now I know this might go without saying but at times we are all guilty of losing touch with reality. This doesn't have to be. So golden rule one is very simple keep your feet on the ground, never forget where you have come from. I believe we must always remember. Remember the feeling of failure, remember how it feels to be alone, remember what it's like to have nothing. Remember what it was like when you needed someone to listen. If we can "remember" it helps us as we go through life. Certain feelings we would never wish to repeat, but empathy is a difficult skill to learn. By remembering you will be able to relate to anyone. We all go through the same emotions just some of us forget or don't want to be reminded who we once were. This is a mistake. Never believe you are above anything or anyone, be non-judgemental. Include others in your thinking and, above all, learn to talk and listen in equal amounts.

Golden Rule Two: Be Selfish

In contrast to the first rule, Golden Rule two is about yourself. Before you can do anything knowing who you are, what you like, dis-like, and your passions is the key to being content. Never expect others to make you happy. Never expect to find happiness in having what you want. Respect money. Respect people. Treat others how you would wish to be treated yourself. Being selfish first is an amazing thing. No guilt, just your personal needs first. You will find the old thinking of putting others before you only works if you have a totally free emotional self. So many use others to base their happiness on. Their dreams and wishes rely on others needing them. When you base your relationships on helping others that's the life you choose. Do not expect others to return the favour or act and think the same way. Most who do this end up lost. If you base your life on yourself first, it's only you who can let you down. It's only you who can be responsible for your happiness. We don't live to serve others even though there are those who would have you think this way. You are living to serve yourself. Once you have mastered rule two then you can enjoy successful relationships that are equal.

Golden Rule Three: Put the work in

This is one of the hardest things for people to understand especially in relationships. So many people talk about wanting a good relationship, "I want to meet my perfect partner" is something I hear every day. But why should you meet your perfect partner if you still have issues and problems? If your last relationship failed ask yourself why? What did I do wrong to make a person who I thought liked me turn away from me. Were they a bad choice? Did they choose me because of how I looked? Or my social profile? Or my image? What was the connection built on? You should be asking yourself these questions at the start of the relationship. Preparing for success is not difficult. You don't need to interview every date you meet for "The job of your partner!" But you must put in the work first. What makes you a good person to date? What are your expectations? Dreams? Agenda? We all have them. Learn about you, self-disclosure, you don't mind sharing, and common ground between you.

Golden Rule Four: Know what you want

Golden Rule Four is simple. Or is it? How many of us really know what we want? We may think we do but I'm not sure why so many of us complicate what we want. Is it because we fear that we will never get anywhere near our hopes and dreams so we make them so far out of reach we could never achieve them? Then there are those of us who believe that we are not good enough, so we set the bar so low we don't ever feel disappointed. The key to knowing what you want is to know yourself. Not what others say about you. Good or bad. But what you think about yourself in your private thoughts. Standards are what we set for ourselves. Others could never set them for us. Why should they? The value we set in ourselves is so very important. If we don't value ourselves who will? We learn very early in life to put people down, it's learnt behaviour from our parents. But because we are what we think once we start this way of thought it's not long before we start doubting who we are. Be the captain of your own ship. Go your own way. Learn it's not good to think in the negative. Whether you think you can or you can't you will be right.

Golden Rule Five: Ask Questions

Never assume. Ask questions. It's not what people say that interests me, it's what they are not saying. In any relationship, we must be prepared to both ask and answer questions honestly. How could we ever know if a person was interested in us? Or what their dreams were? When asking questions, be careful not to interview, or become a machine gunner, firing off question after question. It should always be a balanced exchange. Offer an answer, ask a question of your own. Another thing about asking questions is - never ask a question if you are not going to believe the answer. If you already have a fixed preconceived idea of what you believe, asking questions will only leave you feeling mistrust for the person you are with. Trust is the cornerstone that a relationship is built on. But trust has to be built by understanding, sharing and watching. I think of trust like a China Cup, very easy to break. Be aware of how to accept that we all don't have the same way of thinking and it is possible to change our minds. Try to see relationships as something that evolves. Our needs can constantly be changing so make allowances for your own emotions and those of the people who share our lives.

Golden Rule Six: Know what you can do not what you can't

So many of us focus on what we can't do. Or wish for something that isn't within our reach at that moment. It is such a waste of energy going too far forward in our lives. Worrying is the silent disease of the masses. We go about our daily lives thinking far too far forward. Trying to pre-guess the difficulties we may be facing in the future. We then try to work out a solution. Which, in fact, would be false, because if the problem does arise it is unlikely that it would ever work out the way we thought it might. So when we do encounter problems, it's a good idea to solve them in the moment. Life is complicated enough without adding worries into our thinking about what may happen. Learn the need to live in the moment. We don't know the future; we never will. Anyone who tells you they can predict the future look at their lives see how good they are and how they live. I would say it's not impossible to work out trends from past behaviour, but the only true moment you ever have is right now. It's the only time you can do anything. Make the most of the now, solve the problems in front of you and leave the future well alone.

Golden Rule Seven: Never ever ever give in

How much do you want something? This is a question I always ask people before I teach. I know it's obvious, but I always need to know that when the going gets tough or the subject is difficult that the person I'm teaching isn't going to give in. We can learn anything, do anything if we decide nothing will get in our way. Yes, it may take some longer than others to reach the end but it will happen if we want it enough. Enough to invest our time, enough to push ourselves, enough to dedicate. Without dedication, we will end up giving in. Cutting ourselves short. The key to never giving in is to know what you have a passion for, if you don't enjoy you will give in, if you don't set goals you will give in. But your goals must be realistic to you. You must also do what you do for yourself. If you start something because it's what you want to do, don't let anyone tell you not to. Remember if you can see the benefits from dedication; you will make it to the end.

Thought

Everything you own is only borrowed. You never truly possess anything apart from the love you carry inside your heart. So why do we put so much stock on what we own? Society wants us to create a profile where we strive to own. If we work hard, play the game, then our peers will accept us. We are judged by where we live, the car we drive, the clothes we wear, and what we do as a job.

When you stop and think about it, why would we judge others? Surely we should look at what people stand for, how they speak. Who really cares about television awards or soaps? The world we live in can be very superficial.

Once we start to pull away from what people expect from us or what is lined up for us the world becomes a different place.

Final Thought

Eat, work, sleep, repeat. Do you ever feel each day mirrors the last? The routines we get into shape the day we live. But does life have to be like this? However hard we try we will fall into routines in one way or another, the trick is not to let those routines dictate but let them frame your day so you can do even more. One of my favourite sayings is, "Give a busy person something to do, it will get done". So how we are is how we are if we get used to doing nothing we will want to do less.

I was reading a persons' "Bucket list" all the things they wanted to do before they passed over. Just having one of these lists is a great idea, it acts as a reminder that life doesn't just have to be dull, and it can be as exciting as you want to make it. Do the ordinary well and it creates time to do the extraordinary.

Printed in Great Britain
by Amazon.co.uk, Ltd.,
Marston Gate.